The Derailed Creative

Forward

This work, be it poetry, short stories, excerpts or autobiographical, is dedicated to my battle with anxiety. It is a monster that became my friend before I know the concept of "friend." Although I'm not medicated, there are times when I feel it necessary. My mind becomes foggy, my thoughts interrupted, my words broken before they form. An imaginary weight creeps and sits on my shoulders before I realize it taking form. I want to cry, but I can't. I want to scream, but my mouth won't open. I want to disappear but I can't seem to become ethereal. So I sit, trapped inside a world of my own making, powerless. There are days when I'm void of any emotion except fear and panic. Words and actions can't reach me. I smile to keep the pain just under the surface. Anxiety is a cruel mistress, a devious bastard, and a trifling beast. It does not care that I have things to do, a life to live, and least of all my happiness. It's an abyss lying in wait to suck me in and send me spiraling; descending into the worst parts of myself. These forgotten things swept under a rug and left in an empty room. When it cripples me to the point of becoming numb, I ask myself why. Why does this anxiety exist and persist? How do I get rid of something that feels like an integral part of me? What is the actual source of this bottomless lake? I'm tired of spinning in CIRCLES and vomiting my happiness and confidence! Air becomes so thick with seemingly insurmountable things that, at times, I suffocate. Literally, I find myself at times reminding myself to breathe because I've physically been holding my breath . I close my eyes, inhale, exhale, and repeat as necessary. I'M ALIVE! Or at least I EXIST! The pressure builds until I rage. Quietly at first, but soon, the ugliness tucked away in the crevices of my being escapes and makes itself known, LOUDLY! A proud monster, it does not care who stands before it, consuming good intentions and excreting darkness and vileness. Knowing that its time is limited, it has become skilled at striking and dismantling. Savagery at its best and brightest! As you can see, anxiety is not kind. There are no warnings or rules, just an onslaught of endless negative emotions fighting for dominance, or at least a chance in the light. The root of my anxiety is a journey that I've undertaken to invoke who I really AM. These writings, old and new, are an exploration of theories I have as the source of my anxiety. They are unapologetic and honest in nature. The title, "The Derailed Creative," comes from my realization that my creativity is hindered by my anxiety. So many ideas, stories, poetry and songs were left unfinished as a result of this monster. This beast constantly tells me that my words are stupid and will not be accepted by anyone. I used to lie to myself and say, "I'll finish later." Later has turned into years and I couldn't tell you where some of my works are. Today I decided to sit in front of a lake and plunge into myself. Whether I succeed or fail, my goal is to expel and expand my theories in an effort to increase my mental health. If this work helps anyone, I'll be grateful that I was able to assist someone along their journey. If this is deemed "stupid," I'll be content knowing that I was honest with not only myself but with my heart. Once again, I dedicate this work to my battle with my beastly monster known as anxiety, with the prospect of winning the WAR!

Chapter 1: The Ugly Beast

Self-Doubt (Flogging)

Killing my brilliance is a reflex I abhor,
I can write the prettiest story or poems I adore,
But one wrong very or misunderstanding sends me reeling,
So I self-sabotage to ease and sooth these feelings.
This is easy; I find comfort in destroying my creativity,
It only took once to tell me my words were too complicated, to instill this reassuring negativity.
Creating a machine that chases and wants perfection,
Critiquing small details, plotting to stamp out any insurrection.
Unconsciously, I don't ever mean to criticize or tear down,
It is a projection of my now insecurities, a Freudian slip of my own internal sounds.
What insecurity I'm projecting at any given moment is rooted in my creative ability…
Or inability.
To construct a piece my mind doesn't instantaneously flag as futility.
Even as I write this, I fight the urge to scratch out fragments of my creation,
To revise, rewrite, change my hearts desperate expression.
But I won't this time; I'll finish this masterpiece and present it flawed and raw,
Emotions etched on paper, displayed ragged, unmarred.
My self-doubt has scarred my creativity and creations for as long as I can remember,

Haunted by the ghost of past writings, it treated to leave without so much as a cinder.

It once burned bright, beamed without rhyme or reason, But age, doubt and wounds reduced it to a flicker, only blazing a few time a season.

Before I let it die, I'll create ridiculous rhyme schemes and frivolous stories.

Create imaginary characters and gush over their imaginary glories.

Self-Doubt (The Fear)

Self-doubt is like a lake.
I've been too afraid of crossing it because it's wide, deep, and filled with unknown things.
But as I grow, I'm learning that I don't have to swim across it.
There are many ways to traverse it, and the choice of the vehicle is mine.
Though the lake is filled with unknowns, the doubt that I can cross it subsides knowing that it can be conquered if I choose the right tool.
Creativity is universal but expressing that creativity is an individual experience.
Why did I compare myself to begin with?
My perspective of the world is no less meaningful than anyone else's.

Rainy Day

The smell of rain is in the air!
The sky is this beautiful shade of gray, fascinated, I stare.
What secrets are the clouds hiding to have changed colors so drastically?
Was the sun tired of shining or resting to create a masterpiece?
A loud sound booms from the sky followed by the cracking of a whip.
Wet drops hit my forehead, running down into the crease of my lips.
Suddenly a stream of pellets are pouring from the sky…
I'm in the middle of something exciting.
Turning my face upward, stretching my arms wide, I embrace the wonder invitingly.
I feel it, the masterpiece the sun hid itself to create,
A melody so beautiful, so hypnotic, I don't wish not to escape.
But soon, a voice disbands the melody and I'm plunged from my euphoria,
My body turns without hesitation, recognizing of the pitch and cadence.
"Get inside before you catch a cold"
Momentarily, I weigh my options; think through the consequences of the words that swelled inside my chest,
Discard them quickly as I remember punishment written from these checks,
Begrudgingly, I march inside..
Slowly at first to savor the melody,
But picked up my pace as I noticed patience growing thin at my shuffling steps.

Never again would I stand in a masterpiece crafted by a hidden sun,
I'd watch from inside, warm and dry, listening to the muted song.
That day I learned to fear sky droplets, to fear nature itself
I learned that sunny days are beautiful and rainy days obstruct life.
From that day until now, I've never been able to freely "fall" without rationalizing,
Stuck in a cycle of overthinking and over analyzing.
Never able to fully enjoy things that are breathe-taking and mesmerizing
Because all I knew is scrutiny and criticizing.
All I wanted was freedom on a rainy day.
Instead I was given shelter and a life of gray.

Anxiety

Inhale…
Exhale...
Count to ten,
Then backwards to one again,
Still feel numb?
Pressure in my chest,
Mind racing toward endless possibilities,
Injure me.
Yet I do not protest!
Silently grasping for relief
Told I'm a failure for my unbelief
And all I seek is release.
Blood rushing as my body stiffens
Man or Machine?
Never pausing to check my heart rate…
My current condition
Or if I'm breathing.
Effortless movements mask exhaustion
Persistence pantomimes restlessness
Anxiety

Thoughts

I've exhausted myself to the point where I think I'm crazy…
Seriously!
I don't want to eat, don't want to sleep, don't want to do anything except be.
Void.
Feeling like a piece of empty space occupying space for no reason.
I try to be perfect, be something, be anything to escape my thoughts.
Attempting to immerse myself in noise…all in vain
Once the music stops, once the crowd leaves, I'm once again left alone,
To listen to my thoughts which seem like multiple voices.
Instructing, directing, conflicting, unending, desiring everything from me.
But I fail…because there is nothing left.
Tears will not drain from my eyes,
Will not create a waterfall of pain.
Shall not break through the window to allow misery to join again.
If I could, I'd make this feeling into something I could use,
Instead it's useless, not worthy, just another burden for me to carry.
Please don't tell me that this is life, that this is how I must live,
That this will be my legacy, my story, a treasured tragedy.

I can't go on, this sulfite has met his match,
Lit without a spark of remorse, only a scribbled note attached
Incinerated before I could read it, another piece of me stolen,
Who am I?
What am I?
Where am I?
I try so hard not to feel so lost, feel so confused, and feel so small.
Yet here I am, an ant, an insect without a home, a nomad.
When will it be my turn to smile, to laugh without the weight of the world clouding my skies?
To evolve into the person I know I am, to burn brighter than any star?
Live without a care in the world, dream dreams in peace and serenity.
Breathe without holding my breath; fearing it may not come again.
I want everything, but I can't have anything!
I honestly feel like life is a joke, and I just so happen to have the worst luck!
I DON'T WANT TO BE HERE!
I wish not for death, nor do I wish for sickness, but I wish not to be HERE!!!!
Sadly, I don't know what I mean by HERE.
I just know I don't want to be HERE!
I'm tired of working twice as hard but only getting a quarter of the benefits.
I'm tired of giving people things that I don't HAVE!
I'm not a Savior, I'm not Superman.
I AM NOT AN OBJECT!
I AM ONLY HUMAN!

I feel, I get sad, I feel pain, I AM FLESH AND BONE!
I WANT NOTHING MORE THAN SOMETHING REAL,
SOMETHING I DON'T HAVE TO SHARE!
I WANT TO BE LEFT ALONE!
I WANT TO BE EMBRACED!
I WANT TO NO LONGER BE A ROBOT!
I WANT MY THOUGHTS TO STOP!
They plague me, pain me, eat at me, chain me.
They're too loud too disrupting, too fast, too complex, too insatiable,
They move me, control me, abandon me, desert men
They're argumentative, warring, combative, disengaging, dissatisfied,
THEY ARE MY CRUSHED DREAMS!
THEY ARE MY DISCONTENT!
THEY ARE MY WORLD VIEW!
THEY ARE MINE AND THEY NEED TO
SHUT THE F**K UP!!

Thoughts of the Unknown

Too many ideas travel through my mind,
Pulled into a vacuum and forgotten,
Grasping at lingering memories,
Screaming to reclaim those fades traces,
Watch as the sound slices through barriers of captivity,
Holding.
Attempting to ensnare what I own, to save that which escapes.
Escapes into the deep recesses of my mind
Joining those long forgotten memories of youth
Thoughts move too fast to make sense of the jumble,
Language breaks down, sound becomes silent,
My thoughts have abandoned this being
Why?
How can thought abandon its owner?
What words do I own that I can transform into thought?
Where can I find my lover, my dreamer, the rain dancer?
Thy boy who could dream, who laughed, the fearless one.
He became consumed by society, drained by thoughts, abused by love
He secluded himself within himself and forwarded his life to his shell,
Became careful with his heart, painted a face of fierceness
Cried inside an icebox to freeze and preserve the pain
To remember my misuse and mistakes.

Mama Said

Mama said there would be days like this.
Days of loneliness, bitterness, unpleasantness, and sometimes disappointment.
Mama said there would be days like this.
Nights of restlessness, pillow sweat, and silent agony.
Mama said there would be days like this.
Dreams that dismantle, breakdown, swallow, and reject self-confidence.
Mama said....
See mama said things I didn't understand, things I didn't want to hear, and things that did not validate my existence.
All mama could do was tell, instruct, guide, and attempt to save me from social oblivion.
Her words transformed into echoes, losing conviction as they transitioned.
I wanted to believe them, hold them, and nourish the words until I lived them.
Mama Said…
I wish I would've listened.

Chapter 2: The Lost, Confused and Tired Beast

Who is Self?

I am a stranger to me!
The mirror reflects an alien that mimics my movements.
Its looks like me; it can't be me, but it is in fact ME!
Everyone see this me.
They like this me; He is my pretend to be.
I imitate him to keep up appearances.
The "me" I know is buried behind walls too high and thick I don't bother trying to reach him most days.
So accustomed to giving myself, my WHOLE self to everyone but myself that I'm often dismayed.
I've evolved or devolved…I can't say which; that I can now fully function in an exhausted state.
A state of boredom and emptiness.
I live for the sake of others happiness.
Any happiness I feel is either fleeting or emotionally restricted.
Who is *self*?
I often ask and at times internally scream.
I've been so many things for people that *self* became reclusive and refuses to assert dominance.
Well, that's not totally true… *self* asserts dominance in the most inopportune situations.
He does and acts how he feels, speaks without consideration or hesitation.
Ceding control to *self* is an authentic experience.
He remains true to his truth and is confident in who it is.
Self and I are becoming one again; the process is phenomenal.

Once divorced, we are reconciling our differences and forming a stronger bond.
I've always been stubborn, self-possessed, self-determined and headstrong.
I knew myself and always went my own way.
Those around couldn't handle, didn't like, didn't understand, or refused to understand me.
I wanted to be accepted and not classified and described as *weird*.
I shrank myself.
I held back, pretended I was someone I wasn't.
Beginning the divorce of *self*.
I become an echo of myself, less potent, less effective; distant.
So distant at times I couldn't find my way or answer questions.
Self must have a deep, passionate and overwhelming love for me.
When my anxiety take hold, *self* crashes through my thoughts and reminds me of who I am.
The strength I hold.
That I am POWER itself.
That no matter how insignificant I feel, I MATTER.
Self refuses to allow me to come a whisper, to contain and deny my greatness.
Who is *Self*??
Self is becoming an undeniable force.
I and *Self* and *Self* is I! We will never be separated and belittled again!

Ink Blood

Why can't I write anymore?
Express how I feel?
Construct words with ease; bring rhythmic pleasure to my ears?
I'm stuck
I'm tired, I'm lost...my words no longer exist
They've escaped, fled, and hid themselves from my eyes.
I'm bursting with thoughts, burdened with ideas that I can't touch.
I want to release them, hold them, share them…

My Disposition

This life I didn't choose, it sort of happened,
Tossed into a world of chaos, an urn of endless distraction.
Searching for a relic that I can't begin to visualize,'
Going against the grain, arrogantly hastening my mental demise
Conflicting lies,
Judgmental eyes,
If only I could breathe, intake fresh air and enjoy the sunrise.
Staring at my reflection, I watch myself without expression,
Gaze into my eyes, into my soul, devoid of conceptual protection,
Asking myself who I am and where do I belong

Black Void, Black Water

The waves rose without a trace of wind.
Crashed with claiming sounds and violent echoes.
Lights signaling the presence of boats like stars of the sky,
Blinking in a rhythm, a language that only the truly void understands.
There I stood staring into the nothingness of the night,
Entranced by the black void as the ocean melted into the horizon.
Scary enough to the point of beauty,
Beautiful enough to be called wicked.
So wicked that I called it love
A perfect union of peace and sadness

Chisel

Like a chisel, you meticulously hammer away,
Chipping pieces of my heart and crushing into powder
I watch helplessly, hopelessly, restlessly, unrelenting
Crying silently, drowned in my tears, suffocating.
What have I done?
I've been misunderstood, misheard, misguided for far too long,
I'm empty, void of life to fight another   quarrel
Screaming has no place to reside, emotions have dried.
Functioning to pretend like I'm able to pretend.
Walking as my tears pierce my heart and burn like fire.

Agency

Stolen.
My humanity ripped from my crippled hands.
As I stared in disbelief.
Clutching nothingness like it was breath itself.
Barren and naked, I stood motionless, lifeless, unaware that I'd been taken.
Disillusioned that I was in control, that I owned this body, that I was the "I" of consciousness,
I wandered aimlessly
Wading into imagined shallow waters I swam into depths unknown.
Who was I to question the seemingly predestined roads that lay before me?
To mock plans constructed before my existence?
To exert ownership of my existence?
The desolation of my concept of ownership took away my notion of self.
The oscillation between everyone and nobody became seamless.
Stepping in and out of a foreign body I experienced life's duality.
Being and not simultaneously.

Morning Traffic

I wish these headlights would stop shining!
That my eyes would stop burning and my mind could rest.
I wish these brake lights weren't red.
Reflecting the color of my heart, painting a canvas of pain & rage
I wish I could reach my soul, make a phone call.
Tell it that it will be okay, hoping it believes the lie.
Why does it hurt only when I smile?
Cuts deeper when I laugh though I pretend I control the knife.
My hands are stained with betrayal but I wash them.
Wash them to watch the water swirl in the drain only to be saddened by the permanent stain.
Screaming in silence, breathing without inhaling, I hold my breath…
How long will I survive?
How long can a seemingly soulless body contain years of cries?
The dam is overflowing; each day becomes a game of chess ending in stalemate.
I wait…and wait…and wait…until I surrender.
Yielding to pain, anger, loneliness and misunderstanding,
Watch as tears replay years of agony and sorrow, heartache and jealousy,
Dream that I'm dancing in the rain of freedom,
Only to open my eyes to chains tethered to the past.
Chiseling away at links, breaking bonds that radiate pain so intense my head begins to burn.

I pause…I'm afraid…the unbearable pain creates a new chain.
How do these chains break if they create so much tragedy that I'm consumed and incinerated?

Chapter 3: The Indifferent Beast

Control (Hysteria)

Everything must have a place!
I yearn for categorical, hierarchal, uninhabited space.
Order.
Things in spaces that don't belong get under my skin.
Straining to keep composure I crack like a vase.
My jagged edges cutting before I realize they're exposed,
I panic, desperately trying to repair the damage I've done.
My world is unraveling faster and faster until restraint is gone.
Gripped by hysteria, there is no escape from the "spiral".
This merry-go-round I know all too well…I sit idle.
Trapped within a mental prison because I can't seem to forgive my mistakes,
Can't retract fear-spoken words in my hysterical state.
My peerless, flawless, praised self-control failed and I can't cope.
Chest filling with anxious thoughts, I choke on possibilities that seem plausible in the moment.
Drowning in sorrow as I begin to lament.
Too many times I've been in this place so an emotional response doesn't come,
Only the obsession of my imagined end.

Stamp of Approval

I am not sensitive
But yesterday awakened my sensibilities.
Words hit my ears like fire, scorching the reasonable ideals etched on my heart
Left my mind disconnected.
Swept into a familiar realm of sadness, though I hide the pain.
The world became plain at that moment, clearer than it had ever been.
I learned that decisions are nothing more than a preference.

Doesn't really matter what you've decided; it'll never be good enough.
The person in front of you can tell you what is right and wrong, but never realizes that you have to live…with the choices
You have to stay up soothing regret while caressing misery,
Your voice is nothing but an echo, carried away as the wind blows down your opinion.
Does not my body signify significance?
Does my input matter to the course of my life?
Or am I too dumb to recognize the value of my life?
Have I not fulfilled the requirements to manage my own life?
What must I do to earn, to keep your approval, to remain in your good graces?
I beg of you, tell me so that I won't disappoint you again,
Tell me so that I can sign over my individuality,

Tell me so that I can give you all my passwords, pin numbers, car keys, and whatever else I own,
According to you, I can't navigate this thing called "life".
According to you, I've been wrong since I was born,
According to you, I'm too arrogant and stubborn,
According to you, I'm too difficult,
According to you, I'm too cold-hearted and indifferent
Is this what you wanted, to hear my words of anger and frustration?
To negate my feelings again?
To smile as my heart bleeds?
Standing there with eyes so dark that I can see my reflection in those dead eyes
Suffocating me with fictitious standards and traditional fantasies
Forcing me inside a box that strangles me
Draining the momentum I gained by being an outsider,
Killing the part of me that makes me unique,
Destroying my existence.

Something, Something different

As I move my pen across this paper, it begins revealing my life.
Everything I hold close seems to be running away
Like a hostage with a knife to their throat, I stare blankly, horrified of never being able to go "home"
Impossible to live the life I picture, the life I've painted with a broken brush,
Strokes on the canvas achieved only through effort and will…no technique or skill.
Crippled by inner accusations brought on by socio-religious concepts.
Branded, stained and marked for things I don't understand, things that are beyond my control,
Constantly told to Pray,
Constantly told to Believe,
Constantly told to constantly be told,
I'm tired of this babble, the anecdotes, the verbal bandages that progressively increase the pain
I've Prayed, Believed, Listened, and Betrayed myself for years, yet I'm still no different than before
Questions are no longer relevant, answers are no longer sought, only peace of mind consumes my thoughts,
I've worked without cease, smiled without frowning, laughed to keep agony at bay,
Love…
Love is what led me here, keeps me chasing the seemingly mythical land of happiness

Ask me what I want…Go Ahead Ask Me!
I want ignorant people to shut up and bury their tongues,
Speaking words based on ignorance and close-mindedness only perpetuates the vicious cycle of war, despair, anguish, strife and hatred.
Respectfully disagree, peacefully decline, remove your pride and elevate your thoughts.
Of course this is too much to ask of an arrogant, self-righteous, hypocritical society.
So I'll ask those who have a backbone to stand against society and give the world something, something Different!

Ocean

Sorry...
But I've drowned.
Swept by the tide of everything,
I..LET...GO
Blissfully sinking into nothingness.
Quiet and still.
I'd be lying if I said I resisted and fought.
Instead I made my bed in the sand and awaited the promised solace.
Patiently, unflinchingly, resolved and resigned for the journey.
Building sandcastles with an imagination laced with disappointment and rage.
I sat entertaining myself as the rising tide became visible on the horizon,
Captivate by the tides syncopation, I nearly forgot to take my position.
Body stiff, arms across my chest, grimace permanently affixed.
In an instant, I found myself drowning.
The sensation briefly preceded by the wave crashing so hard I momentarily panicked and screamed for help.
But soon realized I was in the middle of a void without visibility.
The ocean of my emotions was all consuming.
Rendering my sensory organs useless, sending my mind into shock from hypoxia.
But my consciousness remained intact.
Suspended lifeless inside this ocean, I emptied out

Floating Turmoil

These inexplicable emotions have no home!
Yet they fill my bones with rage and pain
Residing just under my skin like an insidious disease,
A parasitic invasion so easy and uncontested.
Lingering love convolutes reality
Manifesting serenity in place of destruction.
Still, these inexplicable emotions have no home
Yet they fill bones with rage and pain.

Vodka & Tequila

I wish I regretted taking those shots but I don't.
I wish I regretted these thoughts but I embrace them.
I wish I felt like this everyday but most days I feel nothing.
Nothing except the void that grows and expands beyond my intent.
Swallowing up every sober thought
Every thought of normalcy
Every thought of belonging
Every thought of self-righteousness and control.
Control...Control...Control
I am powerless to resist this urge for freedom.
This urge to destroy and dismantle,
This urge for complete loneliness.
I am alone and empty.
Poured everything I had into this notion,
Into a picture of safety,
Into something that has evolved into something bigger than I.
My body calls for something I can't seem to grasp.
Wishes for a vapor so toxic, so infectious, so hideous that it'll shred the heart I have left.
A storm is on the horizon and I'm driving into it without my wipers...
Blind but not oblivious.
I wish I regretted those shots but I don't
They make me feel like I'm of this world, like I'm living a life...

Forgotten Commodity

Against the grain I travel without remorse or regard.
Endlessly offering a helping hand and encouraging words while smiling through tear-stained lips.
Forsaking individuality, exhausting resources that have long been exhausted.
Refusing self-service.
Putting the needs of others before my own until I become unknown.
The voice of one has now become the voice of many.
Professing nomadic speeches out of a mouth that does not claim these monologues.
Latching desperately to dreams of being unchained, unburdened, unbroken…undone.
Bursting at the seams like shattering glass…sharp around the edges.
A fragile and fragmented thing I've become, distorted.
Gathering shards of myself feels so natural, so familiar, so…peaceful.
Piece by piece I cherish these serrated objects, basking in their memories.
I carefully reconstruct myself at my workbench, mending the cracks with hope,
Wiping cleans the inside debris with patience, while polishing the outside with self-love.
The work is now complete, and I'm able to face the world again.
Now I realize that I must not be afraid to be authentic, a rebel, a mirror of my inner most thoughts.
Pushing myself beyond limits.
Leeches are a habit I can no longer afford.

For I remember that I am the Forgotten Commodity, and I'm more valuable alive than dead.

Chapter 4: The Loveless Beast

Greeting

When the room is quiet, only in the sound of silence, I think of you.
The ups and the downs, the highs and lows flood my memory,
How I wished that I'd loved you, and I should've been brave enough to admit it.
Pretending to care, two years of wasted words
Memories unreadable.
Lies unexplainable to my heart.
Timing was never right to admit defeat, to break hearts unequally.
Trying but failing to show emotion.
Carried away with promises of better love, uncontrollable feelings wasted.
Lust withered as the winds of change blew, realizing I'd never choose you.
You made it impossible, unreasonable, and unappealing to be wrapped inside your embrace.
To be anchored down with someone so selfishly blind, afraid to live.
Wanting luxury for pennies, pity for anger, and loyalty in place of security.
Broken so you break those who seek to help.
Charge them foolish for their innocence, convict them for honesty, slay them so they'll lie beside you in the bowels of misery.
Perfect I am not, but did I deserve to be treated as an ATM?
Giving currency I didn't possess, overdrawing from my soul.

Your attempted deposits further depleted my account.
Keep your money if you must impose rules.
Count your change until your fingers bleed with remorse and shame.
Then, and only then, deposit them back into that immature heart of yours.
Pity that I reduced myself to being such a spineless and unrecognizable creature for you.
Silver Lining?
The only silver lining I see is the absence of you.
The conclusion of a fable that had no sense of reality.
Falsehoods of adventures you were too ungrateful to appreciate and too broke to finance.
At this point, you will be synonymous with misery and dread.
Don't misunderstand, I don't hate, wish bad, or speak ill of you. Its just…well...
I just think you're too old to be immature, too old to hold grudges, too old to keep making dumb choices, too old to be such an ungrateful little bastard.
Bitter. Spoiled. Insecure.
This is my truth, my story, my words, my version of events.

Window

The window is open,
No need to scream and shout.
My secrets are flying,
Time is not on my side.
Guess I lose this round, this fight, this journey,
Afraid to start again, to change the power of attorney,
Who I am is not the person I am,
My dreams are bigger, larger than my eyes can picture.
The world has altered my perception, corrupted my soul,
Confused, disappointed, and shattered a life that was already complicated.
Searching desperately for intimacy, I twisted love into a joke.
Left trails of broken hearts, without guilt or remorse,
Loving me is too complicated, too confusing, too much to handle,
I'm like water: constantly moving, changing directions, flowing endlessly.
A lonely soul.
The window is open,
And all my secrets are fleeing.
Into my soul through my words,
You're only peeking.

The Losing Game

I suspended time temporarily until I could make a decision,
Looked beyond my inner walls only to face realities vision,
Knowing full well I'd made a mess I continued to indulge my whims,
Without emotions or attachment, without remorse nor regret.
Deluded…maybe…angry no, I just played the game like I did many times before.
Only showing little, if no emotions, displaying a facade of an open door.
Truly I wish I could feel, that my inner being would yearn for another
But it seems impossible when you're your own best lover.
Maybe my standards are too high, my requirements too extreme,
Or maybe I'm destined to be alone and marriage will forever be a dream.
Maybe I've conquered relations, or maybe I've gone insane,
But the moral of the story remains the same
Love exists on a plain that I cannot begin to comprehend,
Inside a universe outside of this time, a symbiotic sin.
Parading its banner, declaring war on hearts,
Taking the pride of many, framing them on a wall of misery.
This is the ballad of love or the battle of love,
I'm profoundly confused,

Swept into a sweet melody, never realizing I was being abused.

…To be loved

My brain hurts because I've silently cried,
I kept my face dry, my eyes open, my heart closed.
The stories spin, the words pierce yet the ending never changes.
I'm always left broken-hearted with chards I can't remove,
Bleeding onto the floor, watching as it spells out "lonely"
How could this happen?
Why does the world laugh at my emotions?
Is it possible for me to love, to hold the heart of another?
I can't fathom the thought of crushing a treasure so precious
But I do.
Without remorse I crumble hearts, smash hopes, and erase dreams
All because I'm not willing to settle, too arrogant to bend, unable to bow,
Is this hubris or just innate stubbornness?
Or is it longing?
Longing to experience the world untainted and unbound,
Unchained, unrestricted, recklessly touching the stars without fearing being engulfed

Vacant Eyes

Your eyes were distant and cold,
But you kissed him.
Lips touching, tongues moving, inhaling passionate breathes.
Yet those eyes are still uninhabited.
Devoid of the affection your lips betray,
Or maybe I'm projecting.
The smile you gave as he walked up the stairs seemed forced but perfected.
How many times have you stood in the mirror and mimed your actions?
Your body speaks love, while your eyes scream escape.
The brim of your hat protects your lover from noticing.
Protects you from having to explain the reflected emptiness,
But prevents you from focusing as I stare attentively, wanting to know your secret.
Searching for meaning in those eyes that remind me of my own.
Are you and I shells of our former selves that loved and no longer can?
Selves moving, smiling, acting as if love still rules our hearts?
Ironically, he sings "Gravity", as he focuses on you with every off key note, though his sincerity makes the song bearable.
Sitting in a chair out of sight, you stared down aimlessly, ignoring his confession, searching the cracks in the floor for meaning.

He went down on his knees, singing and screaming as if pleading for mercy,
Yet your vacant eyes judged and convicted him, though you never looked at him.

Chapter 5: The Beast of Entrapment

The Descent

I've fallen!
Down into a well of complacency!
Chasing pieces of me it never occurred to me that I was descending.
Free falling.
A sweet beginning.
But soon the echoes of my failures resounded.
Searched for footing in these tainted memories, but I was surrounded.
Encamped inside growing walls I clawed desperately
Trying to grasp at anything real, anything pleasant.
As reward for my foolery, I got bloodied hands,
Stained with ignorance or arrogance, doesn't matter which.
All I remember is the pain, the agony, and the beautiful stench.
The smell of something new, something born unexpectedly.
Yet I continued to fall, gathering speed and no change of trajectory.
A scream swell within my throat, but I swallow it like leftover vomit...
A nasty, bitter, acidic reminder.
Recalling all the times I ingested, digested and rejected myself,
To appease and be accepted in a world that doesn't value self.
My silence is a coping mechanism born of societal taught self-hatred.

Always told I was too much, too something, too over animated.
No longer can I see the pieces of myself I was chasing,
Lost sight from the distractions, the self-deprecating.
Practice made perfect,
I can defeat my self-confidence faster than anyone can!
Outwardly pretending to be okay while inwardly using all of my energy to stand,
To be present,
To want to move,
To want to BE!
I believe this is why I embraced the descent.
There was no pressure to be what I'm not,
Do what I can't,
Give more than I have,
Smile when I have no reason,
Forced…
That's the word I've been looking for!
The action I hate the most!
I've felt like a symbiote, my body acting as host.
Doing because I had too, never because I wanted to.
Choosing myself was considered selfish,
Going my own way made me look foolish,
Trying to be myself I looked stupid,
But when I gave up on myself, oddly people approved it.
Shelved myself became ordinary, and "just got through it".
From the sound of my echoes, I think I'm reaching the bottom.
I once feared it, but now I invite it to come.
Sometimes there is no coming up, no place to climb from,

My pieces are at the bottom of complacency and I must get them again.
I'm gathering my self-worth, my self-confidence…a long lost friend.
I'm ready to hit whatever lies ahead,
Nothing can be worse than the life I lived before The Descent.

Theory of Evolution

They say there is no rest for the wicked,
But I'm not sure I'm wicked.
I'm mean, I'm no Angel, but I'm not wicked
So why can't I rest?
My mind is on overdrive and I can't seem to turn it off.
Like a switch was flipped and forgotten.
I sit and ponder why I can't flip the switch or why the switch doesn't work as intended.
It hurts!
Feels like I'm carrying the world inside me.
My words don't reach anyone so they go unspoken,
Buried inside an under-sized casket brimming with all my something's.
The something's I wish were tangible or at least able to be spoken.
I suspect my overdriven state is induced by slow burning anger.
Anger bred from boredom, discontent, fear, or all the rational things I say are irrational.
I've suppressed my feelings so long that I'm not sure I'd recognize them if they appeared.
Everything around me is so aggravatingly normal that I hate it!
There exists no excitement, no spontaneity, no strong desire to do much of anything.
But I suppose I can only blame myself.
I feel trapped inside the cage that I built for safety.
Now it's only a reminder of the limits I imposed on myself.
The "world" I wanted to build is full of nothingness.

A shapeless, monotone blob.
I'm just tired of being everyone's push person when there is nothing within me.
NOTHING!
A husk that moves and pantomimes.
An automaton.
My fear of burning down everything keeps this existence intact.
I'm pretty good at burning and destroying,
Like…an expert on the edge of becoming a pro.
My ability to compartmentalize is dangerous.
I'M DANGEROUS!
Shutting myself down to accomplish anything is something I once took pride in.
Now I understand that makes it easy to detach myself from just about anything.
There is that thing I do subconsciously again:
Point out my flaw and then own up to it in the same breath.
My constant and unwelcome "duty" to make everything okay makes me unfit for life in general.
I have nothing to call my own save a phone and other small knickknacks.
I absolutely have no desire to be bothered.
I know it's a bad and horrid thing to say, but I don't.
The constant drained feeling has reduced my sympathy to about 3 or 4 preset responses.
I'm supposed to care, provide a solution, and be a model son, boyfriend, servant, etc.
And right now, I can't be All because I'm failing at all.
The sad part, I don't really care if I'm failing anymore.
I mean, everyone else's feelings are more relevant than mine, right?

My voice should be an echo but instant it's an overly tired, unenthusiastic, grief laden whisper.
I grieve because the person people see is not who I actually am.
I mean, there are specks of me, but overall it's not me.
Who Am I Really?
Someone who wants the world, someone who doesn't take things too seriously, someone who is scared of everything but doesn't mind trying
Someone who just wanted to fly and see everything,
Who cares too much, who places others before himself?
Who can't "wait to start life"?
Who needs time to figure stuff out?
Who is indecisive because choosing in the moment is stressful?
Who just wants to live the way he wants,
Someone that sometimes dreams so much I lose sight of reality.
I NEED MORE!!
I'm transitioning into this person I don't know,
Like some kind of metamorphosis.
I'd be a liar if I said I didn't like the transition.
I feel more self-aware, self-assured, like I know where I'm going…oh the irony.
This person I'm becoming is unlike any version of me I've ever known.
I think all my current issues are from the fear of this transition.
I'm afraid to let go of who I think I am,
I'm scared that this version of me will destroy the "safety" I've built,
I'm scared that this person will unload my under-sized casket and wave my something's in the daylight.

This person, I fear will burn down everything and be okay living in the ashes.
Or maybe this person will do none of these things and I'm being overly cautious and paranoid.
Either way, this person is coming and I can't do anything about it
Guess this is my Theory of Evolution.

Dark Walls

I sat on my bed with tears in my eyes.
Being alone is better than being with you.
My heart suffocates from the stagnant air.
Body shaking, mind racing, I'm shutting down.
Breathing hurts as my words fall before I speak,
Dark walls.

Small Drop Big Ripple

Finally, I've been released.
The nozzle of the elongated tube has forcefully transformed me into a fraction of myself.
Condensed down into a circular object, reminiscent of a teardrop…irony.
Never once did I ask to be pressed or squeezed, just another part on the assembly line.
Another compartment of a machine that I will never operate, existing to propel an unspecified agenda.
As I descend into a free fall, the scenery below unfolds like paper.
Mass deception spreads like whispering secrets.
Beliefs, deeply wrapped in hatred are presented as ideologies of progress.
Though to confess the bigotry means to accept defeat, to never rise again.
Wars of ignorance and solitude pervade this World like disease.
Infecting innocent minds, corrupting joyous hearts, all for the sake of ego stroking.

Chapter 6: The Hopeful Beast

Defective Manifesto

Normality seems to be measured using antiquated equipment.
We Are Human.
Boastful and Loud yet uniquely created and purposed.
Outside the box we exist, separate but equal.
Dismantling societal norms to live free without boundaries,
Exhausting ourselves to distance ourselves from ancestral standards.
Hammering at chains to change the stains that remain,
Unashamed to speak out names.
Struggling against ideals and traditions made for the select few.

What The Water Gave

Watching the endless blue floor, I pondered the meaning of life.
What it means to love, to be loved, to want love, to need love.
It moved without pretension, made not a boastful presence.
Oscillating, cresting and breaking, fluid and seamless.
A mirror reflecting the humanity I'd forsaken.
Peaceful, so gentle that I could not resist its call.
Washing over me I surrendered with open arms.
Pride notwithstanding, I cracked, giving all I was.
All these demons I held within relinquished their power and found a new host.
Life lessons I found in the water.
Gazing as multiple currents collided and created calm streams,
Like roads in mountains, oil gliding across ice.
These roads do not take away the beauty of the mountain, but join to create something majestic.
An energy transfer of some sort.
The water gave me clarity amongst the confusion.
Blowing the cobwebs from my eyes to present a brand new world.
Allowed me to touch these things I was too afraid to grasp.
Taught fundamental lessons on the significance and interconnectedness of events.

The water gave me ambition to accomplish goals and continue to reach
To believe in the soul that is uniquely me, and stop compromising.
Assured me that God exists and still works wonders.
Professed to me that Life is ever-changing and that I have to release the stress,
The water gave back the voice I thought I'd lost.
The sound that is undoubtedly me,
The eyes to see beyond what the eye can see
What the water gave is a fresh mind with ideas to change my life.
What will you do with what the water gave?

Expanse

Over the crest of my tears, the sun shines on new land.
A beautiful meadow sprouted from my wells.
Watered with bitterness, anguish, disappointment and disbelief.
Created out of a broken existence filled with hope.
Decorated in jubilant colors despite the creators' choice of pastel shades.
My hands are moist from wiping my eyes,
My face glistens with salty residue, but I am captivated.
As my vision clears, the birds sing forgotten melodies
Words that my heart had long released, words I was too afraid to speak.

Whisper

I heard a voice carried by the wind.
It never spoke.
Only wrapped itself around this phantom, a broken man.
Soothing pain that accumulated over years, healing a compromised heart.
The wind elevated the mind of a dreamer who could no longer dream.
Mental scars dripping with judgment ran deeper than visible.
Heart…ache.
The gentle breeze calmed the storm, dispelled the clouds, and seared the chains of bondage.
Separated reality and fantasy, brought back hope to this hopeless soul.
Reclaimed thoughts of success, conquering unrevealed fear.
Wall's of hurt,
Transformed into a hurricane of Hope.

Made in United States
Orlando, FL
10 February 2025